DON'T LOOK NOW

Daphne du Maurier's

DON'T LOOK NOW

Adapted for the stage
by Nell Leyshon

OBERON BOOKS
LONDON

WWW.OBERONBOOKS.COM

First published in this adaptation in 2007 by Oberon Books Ltd
521 Caledonian Road, London N7 9RH
Tel: +44 (0) 20 7607 3637 / Fax: +44 (0) 20 7607 3629
e-mail: info@oberonbooks.com
www.oberonbooks.com

A catalogue record for this book is available from the British
Library.

PB ISBN: 9781840027303
E ISBN: 9781849437196

Visit www.oberonbooks.com to read more about all our books
and to buy them. You will also find features, author interviews and
news of any author events, and you can sign up for e-newsletters
so that you're always first to hear about our new releases.

Characters

JOHN

LAURA

SISTER

BLIND SISTER

RESTAURANT PROPRIETOR

CLERK

POLICE CHIEF

DWARF / CHILD

All other parts are doubled with the Restaurant Proprietor,
Clerk and Police Chief.

Dialogue in square brackets is spoken in Italian.

This adaptation of *Don't Look Now* was first performed on 22 February 2007 at the Sheffield Lyceum, produced by Sheffield Theatres and transferring on 13 March 2007 to the Lyric Hammersmith, with the following company:

Karen Anderson

James Bellorini

Simon Paisley Day

Eliot Giuralarocca

Joanna McCallum

Enzo Squillino

Susie Trayling

Susan Wooldridge

Conceived and Directed by Lucy Bailey

Designer Mike Britton

Lighting Designer Chris Davey

Original Music and Sound Design Nell Catchpole & J Peter Schwalm

Voice Coach Penny Dyer

Fight Director Richard Ryan

Casting Siobhan Bracke

A massive thank you to director Lucy Bailey. This adaptation is the result of our creative working relationship.

N.L.

Act One

A choir: English music, young male voices.

Underneath the singing, the sound of funeral bells emerges.

The music loses its Englishness and becomes Italian.

RESTAURANT, TORCELLO

LAURA sits at her table, writing a postcard to Johnnie. JOHN is reading a local Italian paper. LAURA hesitates, pen poised, forming a sentence.

The SISTER and her BLIND SISTER are at their table.

JOHN lowers his paper, watches.

The SISTER is studying the menu. The BLIND SISTER stares towards JOHN, who becomes very aware of her gaze.

JOHN taps LAURA's postcard to get her attention. LAURA looks up.

JOHN: Don't look now.

> *LAURA goes to look.*

> I said don't look now. There are a couple of old girls over there.

> *JOHN nods in their direction. LAURA waits, then turns and sees. She looks back at JOHN.*

> Well?

LAURA: They're marvellous.

JOHN: They are, aren't they?

LAURA: John. Are you sure they're old girls?

JOHN: Go on.

LAURA: They look like men in drag.

JOHN: (*Laughs.*) Of course. Men in drag.

> *WAITER interrupts, sees LAURA hasn't finished.*

WAITER: Is everything all right?

LAURA: Oh yes. Delightful. I'm just rather full.

WAITER: And you, sir?

JOHN: Molto bene, grazie.

WAITER: My pleasure. Sir. Lady.

WAITER leaves.

JOHN: This insistence on speaking English. Honestly it drives me absolutely potty.

LAURA: Poor man. He only wanted to *praticare* his English.

JOHN: They should appreciate my making an effort.

LAURA: You just hate being a tourist.

JOHN: True.

What have you written?

LAURA holds up the postcard, reads.

LAURA: 'Darling Johnnie, Daddy and I are in Torcello, on a day trip out of Venice. Work hard and good luck in the match.'

I don't know what else to say.

JOHN: Just put, 'Love, Mummy'.

LAURA: No. There must be something else. Something I need to say.

LAURA thinks of what to write.

JOHN starts reading his paper again.

The SISTER helps the BLIND SISTER with her napkin.

LAURA gives up thinking of what to write, looks up at JOHN.

What's happening in the outside world?

JOHN: Oh this and that. A furore about the gondoliers' wages, a missing cat, that kind of thing.

LAURA: A missing cat?

JOHN: Cat, yes.

LAURA: Are you sure you can read it?

JOHN: Of course I can. It says here 'gatto'. Cat.

LAURA: It's just you're quite rusty.

JOHN: Rusty? What d'you mean, rusty?

LAURA: Well you haven't used it for a while, darling.

JOHN: I can slip straight back into it. Just a question of getting your ear in. Look here. (*Showing.*) There's a photo of a cat.

LAURA: All right. I believe you.

JOHN: Good. Or I'll really embarrass you and ask the waiter how rusty he thinks I am.

LAURA: Oh no, please don't.

JOHN: Or I could ask one of the old girls over there.

LAURA: No.

JOHN: I could serenade her in my perfect Italian. (*Sings quietly.*)

LAURA: Stop it, John.

JOHN looks at the SISTERS.

JOHN: Don't look now but one of them is staring at me.

Quite a way she has with it. They do stand out to high heaven.

Do you think she's trying to hypnotise me?

LAURA goes to turn.

Don't be too obvious, darling.

LAURA drops her napkin, turns and sees. She turns back and, half laughing:

LAURA: They're definitely men.

JOHN looks at them, stifles a laugh in his napkin.

JOHN: God, you're right.

What would you say they're doing here?

LAURA: I'd say they're criminals.

JOHN: That's it! Criminals.

LAURA: They're doing the grand European tour. Staying in fine hotels.

JOHN: And they alternate between being men and women.

LAURA: Yes.

JOHN: Twin sisters today on Torcello, twin brothers tomorrow in Venice. It'll be wigs off, trousers on.

LAURA: Jewel thieves or murderers?

JOHN: Murderers definitely.

Oh God, she has her eye on me again. Why me?

LAURA looks again.

LAURA: No, no. It's me she's staring at.

They're sizing up my neck, maybe checking for my pearls. So they're jewel thieves, not murderers.

JOHN: Of course we could be completely wrong.

LAURA: Ah. What if they're just a couple of retired schoolmistresses on holiday?

JOHN: They share a house together.

LAURA: In Wiltshire. They've saved up their whole lives to come to Venice.

JOHN: They could be dog breeders. Maybe they show them, running round the ring with their pugs.

LAURA: Pugs, of course.

JOHN: With short legs and ugly little faces.

LAURA: Yes, and they talk to them, hold out a biscuit. Say come to Mummy, my little baby.

JOHN: God, what a thought.

JOHN laughs. Pause.

LAURA: You know that food was really very good. It's been a lovely lunch.

JOHN takes LAURA's hand.

JOHN: Good. I've enjoyed it too. I'm so glad we chose to come away. It's so lovely to see you like this. Like you again.

LAURA looks away. Takes her hand away.

LAURA fiddles with the postcard, writes something, crosses it all out quite violently. Screws up the card.

Don't. Darling, what are you doing?

LAURA: Nothing.

JOHN: What is it?

LAURA: 'Darling Johnnie. Work hard and good luck in the match.'

Such a stupid thing to write.

JOHN: It's not stupid.

LAURA: It is, John. It's facile. Stupid empty words.

JOHN: Laura.

No response.

JOHN watches as LAURA takes another card and starts again.

LAURA: Do you think Johnnie will ever come to Venice?

JOHN: Everyone comes eventually. What is it they say? In Venice the whole world meets.

LAURA: I was just thinking of Johnnie back at school. Wondering what he's doing. If he is all right.

JOHN: You think of him too much. Anyway you know it's the best place for him. With his friends, safe as houses.

LAURA: Maybe. Maybe.

John.

LAURA hesitates.

JOHN: What?

LAURA: I don't know.

No. I do.

Last week I met a woman I hadn't met before.

JOHN: Who?

LAURA: It doesn't matter who she is. The point is we got talking and she asked me how many children I had.

I didn't know what to say. She waited for me to respond, but I really didn't know what to say. I couldn't say one. But I knew if I said two, she would ask me about them.

And so I had to tell her what had happened to Christine.

Then there was this terrible silence when she didn't know what to say.

I realised you can't tell people. You have to protect them from hearing it. It hurts too much.

And yet not telling makes me feel so unutterably lonely.

Pause.

Have you nothing to say?

JOHN: What can I say?

LAURA: I don't know.

Pause. Eventually JOHN clears his throat and reads his paper.

LAURA turns and watches the SISTERS, who are eating, the SISTER helping the BLIND SISTER. LAURA turns back to say something to JOHN, but the paper is between them.

John.

JOHN lowers the paper.

What are you reading about?

JOHN: Nothing.

JOHN folds the paper.

Did you want anything else to eat or drink?

LAURA: No.

There is a disturbance as the SISTER stands.

JOHN: Don't look now, but one of our old girls is going to the loo. (*Whispers.*) Do you think she is going to change wigs?

LAURA: She may have a suitcase hidden in there.

Pause while the SISTER passes their table.

I need to go as well. I'll follow her and see what I can ascertain.

LAURA goes to get up.

JOHN: Be careful.

LAURA: Yes. Supposing she starts to strip in there.

JOHN: Just be sure she doesn't have a syringe and try to knock you out.

LAURA tries not to laugh.

LAURA: I simply must not laugh in there. And if we come out together, do not look at me.

LAURA stands and picks up her bag.

Wish me luck.

LAURA follows the SISTER to the bathroom.

JOHN pours himself the rest of the wine and sits back, smokes, waits.

The BLIND SISTER stares at JOHN.

JOHN becomes increasingly uncomfortable. He stares back, but she continues to stare and he stubs out his cigarette. Calls the waiter.

JOHN: Il conto.

WAITER: The bill, certainly sir.

JOHN stands, impatient, and walks towards the bathroom, then returns to the table. The BLIND SISTER continues to stare.

The WAITER returns with the bill.

Was everything satisfactory, sir?

JOHN: Assolutamente.

JOHN takes money out, leaves a tip.

WAITER: Thank you.

JOHN: Prego.

WAITER: Enjoy your holiday, sir.

JOHN: Grazie.

The other SISTER returns from the bathroom, touches BLIND SISTER on her shoulder. They move away, arm in arm. JOHN watches, does not see LAURA return at first.

JOHN turns, sees LAURA.

I must say you took your time.

Hesitates as he sees her.

LAURA bumps into a chair, nearly falls.

Darling. Sit down.

JOHN pulls a chair out, sits her down. The WAITER comes to help.

WAITER: Is she all right?

JOHN: Thank you, but she's fine.

WAITER: Are you certain?

JOHN: Absolutely. She'll be fine.

WAITER: Sir.

WAITER withdraws.

JOHN: Darling, what is it? Tell me – are you ill?

*LAURA shakes her head. Turns and looks at him. Her face changes
and she moves from being dazed to being exalted.*

LAURA: Oh, John.

JOHN: What is it? Whatever has happened?

LAURA: (*Slow.*) It's quite wonderful. The most wonderful thing
that could possibly be.

JOHN: What?

LAURA: John. She isn't dead, she's still with us.

JOHN: What are you saying?

LAURA: The reason the sisters kept staring at us. They could
see Christine.

They could see her.

John. Did you hear me? They could see Christine.

JOHN: Laura.

LAURA: She was wearing her party dress. She described her to
me. Exactly how she was.

JOHN: Laura, stop.

LAURA: (*Not hearing.*) We stood washing our hands at the
basin, then she just turned to me.

She said, don't be unhappy any more. Just like that. Don't
be unhappy any more.

JOHN: Laura, come on, darling

LAURA: No, John. You have to listen to me.

She said to me, my sister has seen your little girl. Her
sister, you see, is psychic. She has studied the occult all

her life, but since going blind she has had real visions.
She really sees things, like a medium. And she could see
Christine, she said she was at the table with us. Sitting right
between us. Imagine. Right between us.

JOHN: Oh, Laura. There was no one at the table. No one.

Look.

You see, nothing.

You must stay calm, darling. You mustn't wind yourself
into a state.

LAURA: But don't you see, I'm not in a state. For once I am
not in a state. Something has changed.

I did think when she told me, that I would faint.

But she understood. She said something like the moment
of truth and joy was as sharp as a sword and that was how
it felt.

She told me not to be afraid, John, and I'm not. I'm really not.

Oh, John. Don't look at me like that. I swear I'm not
making it up. It's all true.

JOHN: Darling, of course I believe you. I'm just upset that
you're upset.

LAURA: But I'm not upset. I'm not at all. You see, I am happy.
So very very happy.

All those weeks at home have been hell.

JOHN: I know.

LAURA: While we've been here, I've tried to hide it from you.
I haven't really talked about it.

The finality of it all was just unbearable. But now it's as
though her dying isn't the end.

Suddenly I can remember her as she was, not when she
was ill. That's all I've been able to think of, her ill. And us
unable to help her, unable to do anything.

LAURA gets a tissue from her bag, blows her nose.

I know the woman was right. I know it. You see, she described her just as she was at her birthday party, with her red dress. Her little red shoes. And she was smiling, happy. Oh darling, I'm so happy I think I'm going to cry.

You see, there's nothing to worry about any more.

Do you have a cigarette?

JOHN gets her a cigarette and lights it.

You do believe me?

JOHN: (*Hesitates.*) Well, yes, but there's always an explanation for these things.

LAURA: What explanation? She saw her. I know it.

I mean, how would she know what Christine was wearing? How could she describe her to me? Down to the colour of her dress. She could even see the six candles on the cake.

Answer me that. How could she?

JOHN: There's always an explanation for these things.

LAURA: And? What can it be?

LAURA waits.

You see.

JOHN: You say the sister was blind?

LAURA: Blind, yes.

That's why she has the visions. You understand, she can see things we can't.

There are things there that we can't see. There is more than just this.

JOHN: Maybe.

LAURA: No. Not maybe.

Oh, John.

LAURA takes JOHN's hand.

JOHN: Laura.

You didn't arrange to meet them again?

LAURA: No. Why should I?

There's nothing more to know. She had her wonderful vision and I now know Christine is happy, and that is the end of it.

JOHN: Is it?

LAURA: Yes. The end of it.

They're moving on soon, anyway. That's what's funny, it is a little like our game, they are going round the world. But I don't think they are murderers or thieves.

LAURA stands. JOHN goes to help her.

There's no need. I'm absolutely fine. In fact I'm more than fine. I really do feel quite quite different.

JOHN: Do you want to go back to Venice, to the hotel?

LAURA: Why?

JOHN: I thought maybe a lie-down or something.

LAURA: I thought we were going to see the Cathedral. That's why we came to Torcello.

JOHN: Of course.

LAURA: Oh, John.

This happening has changed everything. You know that, don't you?

It's changed everything.

LAURA and JOHN move and enter the following scene, and we are in:

18

CATHEDRAL, TORCELLO

A vast space. A Madonna and child against gold. JOHN looks at the size of it all, taking it in. JOHN holds the Michelin guidebook.

LAURA goes to the candles, lights one, adding to the mass of them.

JOHN, his back to the Madonna, looks up at the mosaic in front of him, checks the book, looks up again. He calls out.

JOHN: Laura. Darling.

> You have to see this. Look. It's quite extraordinary.
>
> *LAURA approaches.*
>
> It is, isn't it? Extraordinary.
>
> *No response.*
>
> Are you all right, darling?

LAURA: I'm fine. I was lighting a candle for Christine. I said a small prayer.

JOHN: And you're all right?

LAURA: Honestly, darling. Don't fuss.

JOHN: No.

> *LAURA looks up at the mosaic.*

LAURA: It is stunning.

> *JOHN holds out the open book, but LAURA does not take it.*

JOHN: Do you want to read about it?

LAURA: No. I'll read it later.

JOHN: It does put one in mind of Dante's inferno. Fascinating to see how they were trying to make sense of the world.

> It really was worth the trip.
>
> *LAURA turns, sees Madonna and Child, cries out.*

LAURA: Oh.

She steps forward, looks. JOHN reads his book.

JOHN: Amazing to think over twenty thousand people lived on Torcello. Now there can't be much more than twenty. They destroyed a lot of buildings, recycled them for Venice. We're so lucky this remains.

LAURA: Do look at this.

Look at her.

JOHN: They really did desert it in droves.

LAURA continues to look at the Madonna.

No wonder Torcello has two stars. Unlike that disappointing little place yesterday. No. There's no doubt they got it right here.

While LAURA has her back to him, JOHN sees the SISTERS arrive.

BLIND SISTER stares at him.

LAURA: John. Look at this.

JOHN: What?

LAURA: Darling, please look.

JOHN quickly stands between LAURA and the SISTERS.

Look at her. She's so beautiful. So happy. Serene.

Quite beautiful.

There's some magic quality about her. Something not of this world. It goes right through one.

JOHN is looking at the SISTERS, repositioning himself. The BLIND SISTER reacts as she sees her vision. SISTER holds her.

John. Don't you feel it too?

John. Are you listening?

JOHN: I'm sorry.

LAURA: What is it?

JOHN: I'm just not sure I want to be here. Shall we go?

LAURA: We've only just arrived. I thought you wanted to see it. You talked about it enough.

JOHN: It's so hot.

LAURA: (*Laughing.*) But it's far hotter outside, silly. It's cooler in here.

Does it say anything in there about the Madonna?

JOHN doesn't respond.

There was a painting in the school chapel, very like this, and I used to look at it, wonder what it felt like to have a child.

I knew I wanted a child from very young.

JOHN looks up at the SISTERS, who are leaving.

I don't know how you know, but you do. Such an instinctive thing. I wonder if it's just women.

Did you always want children, John?

I often think of Johnnie in his school chapel. Do you think he sits in the very same seat you sat in?

No response.

I wonder if he has faith. I'd like to think he has some comfort, but he has never said. I suppose I'll know less and less what he thinks as he gets older.

JOHN: I need to get out.

SISTERS leave.

LAURA: What?

JOHN: It's just suddenly all rather oppressive.

LAURA: What do you mean?

JOHN: All that gold on the walls. Look. All that gold.

LAURA: What an odd thing to say.

JOHN: I really feel I can't breathe. I really can't. I need to get out.

LAURA: Oh.

JOHN: Now.

LAURA: What a shame, we may never come again.

JOHN: I'm sorry.

LAURA: Do you want to go back to Venice?

JOHN: Can we just please go and get some air?

LAURA: All right. Come on, then.

How funny. It's me looking after you now.

LAURA takes JOHN's arm. They move to the outside world, and we are in:

TORCELLO

JOHN and LAURA are by the water.

LAURA: John, darling.

JOHN turns back.

I don't think this leads anywhere much.

JOHN: It's just good to be outside.

Let's sit down.

JOHN pulls LAURA and sits down.

He looks at the water. LAURA takes the guide book.

LAURA: There's a lot to see still. There's the museum, the Santa Fosca.

JOHN: I don't need to see it.

JOHN takes the book and puts it down.

It's the wrong time of day for sight-seeing, anyway.

LAURA: I suppose.

JOHN: Come on. Sit down with me.

JOHN places his arm around LAURA. They sit a while.

LAURA: Are you feeling better?

JOHN: I am.

LAURA: Good.

They sit, contemplate.

JOHN: What an act of extreme folly.

LAURA: What?

JOHN: This whole thing. Venice, Torcello, all of this. When you think what humans need. Warmth, dry conditions.

And they built here, it's rather pathetic. Doesn't stand a chance.

LAURA: I wonder why they built here.

JOHN: You can feel the damp in the air. The buildings soaking up the water.

LAURA: Maybe they thought they were beavers.

JOHN: What?

LAURA: Well, all of them running round gathering materials, building and damming.

JOHN: I like that. Beavers.

LAURA: Silly little men with their beaver moustaches.

JOHN: (*Laughing.*) Brown beaver moustaches.

LAURA: But it is all so beautiful.

JOHN: Undeniably. It's all a beautiful folly.

LAURA: John.

Do you remember that time we went to the zoo and Johnnie and Christine were watching the beavers.

JOHN: You have beavers on the brain.

LAURA: I do, don't I?

They started to play and it looked like they were really fighting. Christine started to cry. Johnnie too.

JOHN: I don't think he did cry.

LAURA: He did.

JOHN: He didn't.

LAURA: He did, John. He just wouldn't have let you see.

That was a lovely day.

JOHN: It was, yes.

LAURA yawns, leans on JOHN.

LAURA: That's the trouble with lunch. Makes one so sleepy.

JOHN: Put your head here. (*Pats lap.*) I won't mind. I'll watch over you.

LAURA: In case the beavers come?

JOHN: Exactly.

LAURA: Protect me from their grisly teeth.

JOHN pretends to be a beaver, biting. LAURA laughs.

Don't.

JOHN kisses the top of LAURA's head, rests his head there.

JOHN: Are you glad we came?

LAURA: I am. And you?

JOHN: Of course.

LAURA: Good.

Pause.

John.

JOHN: Yes.

LAURA: Do you think Christine is sitting here beside us right now?

Pause. JOHN looks away, removes his head from hers.

Do you?

JOHN: Do you?

LAURA: I do, yes.

JOHN: I see.

LAURA: Do you think she is?

JOHN: (*Slow, reluctant.*) I expect so. If you feel she is.

LAURA: Oh, I do feel it. I do.

An extraordinary thing has happened to me. You see, after it all, I was left with that image of her so ill with the meningitis. This dreadful memory which I would replay in my head over and over.

When you picked her up and carried her to the car. I could see her head hanging down, floppy. Her dark hair trailing. And I could see her little legs, her bare feet.

JOHN stands.

JOHN: Laura. Please don't. I don't want to hear any more.

LAURA: But I have to tell you this one thing.

JOHN: You don't, actually.

LAURA: But I do, John. You see, I haven't been able to think of anything other than the present tense. I couldn't bear to remember the past, because of what happened, couldn't bear to think of facing the future without her, but now I can. It's as though time has opened up for me. And I can finally move into the future, now I know she is with us.

LAURA jumps to her feet. She goes to leave.

JOHN: Where are you going now?

LAURA: To get the ferry.

JOHN: Oh. Can't we catch a later one?

LAURA: Why? We ought to get back.

JOHN: Are you planning to go and find the sisters again?

LAURA: Why did you say that?

JOHN: No reason.

LAURA: John.

JOHN: Well, you've had quite enough excitement for one day.

LAURA: Don't be silly, John.

I only wanted to see if there's a little something on one of the stalls to take back for Johnnie. I could post it to school.

JOHN: Right.

LAURA: So are you coming? Or are you staying here? I'll leave you to the beavers?

JOHN: I'm coming. But only if I can buy you something from the stalls. Can I?

LAURA: Oh, darling, I don't need anything. No, nothing.

You see, I have absolutely everything I need.

LAURA takes JOHN's hand and they leave.

HOTEL, VENICE

The POLICEMAN takes his photographs back.

POLICEMAN: [Call me as soon as you hear anything.]

CLERK: [Of course.]

POLICEMAN: [Don't hesitate. You understand.]

CLERK: [Why would I? They're our tourists too. I have to go.]

CLERK sees JOHN and LAURA enter, carrying shopping bags and two baskets.

POLICEMAN: [Good afternoon.]

CLERK: [Good afternoon.]

POLICEMAN leaves.

The CLERK gives JOHN the room key.

Welcome back to Venice.

JOHN: Thank you.

CLERK: And Torcello, she was beautiful?

LAURA: Just as you said.

CLERK: But not as beautiful as Venice?

LAURA: How could it be? Nothing is as beautiful as Venice.

CLERK: Ah, it makes me happy when you say that.

Gestures at bags.

You have been shopping?

JOHN: Yes. Multi saccos. La Signora.

You know what women are like.

LAURA: John.

CLERK: My wife, she loves shopping also. We are having a baby soon, and she has so many things. Too many.

LAURA: How lovely. Your first baby?

CLERK: Yes. I am a very proud man. Nervous also.

LAURA: When will it be born?

CLERK: The doctor, he says in one month.

LAURA: And is your wife well?

CLERK: Very well. Thank you.

You need help with these bags to your room? You buy a lot of things.

JOHN: As I said, you know what women are like. But we can manage. Thank you.

27

LAURA: Yes. Thank you.

CLERK leaves and we are in the bedroom.

VENICE HOTEL ROOM

JOHN places the bags on the bed.

We hear music through the open window.

LAURA: John. You are terrible. (*Laughing.*)

JOHN: What?

LAURA: You know what. Blaming me for all the bags and shopping. I told you I didn't need anything.

JOHN: I know, but I wanted to buy you some things. I don't care what you think.

LAURA: But you care what he thinks. You want him to believe it was me.

JOHN: Of course.

LAURA: 'You know what women are like.' Honestly. You are beastly.

LAURA undoes a bag.

Three scarves. So excessive.

LAURA takes them from the bag.

They are beautiful.

JOHN: Of course they are. They have to be, if they're to grace your head.

JOHN strokes her hair and holds LAURA's head in his hands and kisses her. They embrace.

LAURA: It's been a lovely day. I shall never forget it, ever.

JOHN: Good.

LAURA: And I can at last begin to enjoy our holiday.

JOHN: I'm so pleased.

LAURA lays out clothes on the bed, checks them against the headscarves. JOHN watches.

So in this new mood of enjoyment, where would you like to eat tonight?

LAURA: I don't know. You?

JOHN: I want you to choose.

LAURA: What are the choices?

JOHN: Well there is always the usual.

LAURA: Or?

JOHN: Or we could be daring and try somewhere new.

LAURA: We've already spent too much today.

JOHN: I don't care. Honestly, you're too easy to please.

LAURA: Darling, don't complain. I could be one of those demanding wives. Asking for the new season's dresses. A new motor car.

JOHN: God forbid.

LAURA: So be grateful I'm easy to please.

JOHN: I am.

JOHN looks round the room.

How odd to think this room will still be here when we've gone.

I don't want it to be anyone else's. It feels like it should always be ours.

LAURA: Is that just this particular room? Or all hotel rooms we've had?

JOHN: I don't know.

No. It is more with this one, just the feeling of it all, us being here. Right now, in this moment. I don't know. I'm not making sense, am I?

LAURA: You are, actually.

Pause.

Some poor woman will have to come and tidy it when we're gone.

JOHN: Yes. She'll have to make it anonymous again, wipe out our memory for the next load of tourists.

LAURA: And you know who'll be next in the room?

JOHN: Who?

LAURA: The man we saw on the ferry, the very thin one with the vast wife.

JOHN: No.

LAURA: Yes.

Do you think they are lovers, meeting clandestinely?

JOHN: What do you think?

LAURA: I think he has a too thin wife at home and has always wanted a woman like that, and he rests his head on her enormous bosom.

JOHN: Oh my God.

Laura. Don't look now but they're on the balcony.

LAURA looks, laughs.

LAURA: John. You are terrible.

My heart nearly stopped.

JOHN: Come here.

JOHN embraces LAURA.

So where shall we go to eat?

LAURA: Shall we be dull and stay here?

JOHN: I'd like to go out.

LAURA: Then we shall.

JOHN: I can't quite face all those dreary couples and the silence in the dining room.

Anyway I feel like getting sloshed.

LAURA: It's not going to be bright lights and music, is it?

JOHN: I was thinking about an intimate little place. Let's find some dark cellar full of married women and their lovers.

LAURA: We know what that means.

JOHN: What?

LAURA: You'll be making eyes at some young Italian lovely, and I'll be staring at a man's back.

JOHN: (*Laughing.*) Or the other way round, you'll be catching the eye of the waiter, I'll be trapped by matrons.

Let's just wander round and find somewhere we like the look of.

LAURA: Then what shall I wear? What do you think of this?

LAURA holds up a dress.

JOHN: Is it new?

LAURA: John. You know it isn't.

JOHN: Oh dear.

LAURA: Or I could wear the blue. Oh I don't know. No maybe this one.

Shall I try it on? Will you tell me honestly what I look like?

JOHN: Of course.

LAURA takes off her clothes, stands in her slip and bra.

Don't put it on. Not yet.

LAURA: No.

JOHN: Laura, darling.

LAURA looks at him.

Please.

LAURA says nothing and JOHN steps closer. He takes her in his arms and lays her gently on the bed, like a child. Peels off her stockings.

There. Nothing to worry about.

My lovely lovely little Laura.

So beautiful.

So so beautiful.

As JOHN and LAURA make love, we see the SISTERS in their pensione, getting ready for the evening, the SISTER helping with the BLIND SISTER's clothes.

We hear them repeating words, practising their Italian verbs.

SISTER: *Sono, sei, è.*

BLIND SISTER: *Sono, sei, è.*

SISTER: *Siamo, siete, sono.*

BLIND SISTER: *Siamo, siete, sono.*

SISTER: *Sono, sei, è.*

BLIND SISTER: *Sono, sei, è.*

SISTER: *Siamo, siete, sono.*

BLIND SISTER: *Siamo, siete, sono.*

SISTER: *Sono, sei, è. Siamo, siete, sono.*

BLIND SISTER: *Sono, sei, è. Siamo, siete, sono.*

LAURA gets out of bed and wanders round the room, tidying and pottering. JOHN watches from the bed, then closes his eyes.

LAURA leaves the room and we hear water running.

As JOHN sleeps we still see the SISTERS.

BLIND SISTER stops and stands, rigid. JOHN turns in bed, as though she has entered his inner sleeping world.

LAURA re-enters, dressed, fixing her earrings, and shakes JOHN, who wakes startled.

LAURA: Darling. Darling.

JOHN: What?

LAURA: You dropped off.

Gosh, you look like you've had a fright.

JOHN: Do I? I was dreaming.

LAURA: What about?

JOHN: Oh nothing.

LAURA: Come on.

JOHN: No. It was nothing.

How odd. It felt like I was asleep for an age.

God, darling, you do look beautiful.

LAURA: Thank you.

JOHN: Come here.

JOHN embraces and kisses LAURA.

Are you all right?

LAURA: Yes. Why?

JOHN: I'm sorry. You know. Earlier. It had been a long time.

LAURA: Oh, John. Don't say that. You know it was lovely.

JOHN: Yes, but –

LAURA kisses JOHN to silence him.

LAURA: I said it was lovely. It always is.

Now come on, go and get dressed.

JOHN leaves.

We see the SISTERS finish getting ready and they also leave.

LAURA speaks, as though to Christine.

Nothing to worry about.

My lovely, lovely little Christine.

So beautiful.

So, so beautiful.

VENICE STREET

JOHN and LAURA stand in the street.

LAURA: John, darling. I swear we've come in a circle.

JOHN: We haven't.

I tell you we're almost at the public gardens where they hold the Biennale.

LAURA: We're nowhere near there.

JOHN: Of course we are. It just looked different in daylight.

LAURA: We don't want to get lost this late. The place is like a maze.

JOHN: Don't fuss. We're fine.

LAURA: I don't like the look of it.

JOHN: Look, I have an instinct for these things.

LAURA: It's not that way. I know it's not.

JOHN: Of course it is.

LAURA: Let's turn back, John. I really don't like it here.

JOHN: Let me try and look at the map again.

JOHN pulls the map out, tries to see it in the dark.

We hear a scream.

LAURA: What was that?

JOHN: I don't know.

LAURA: John. What was it?

JOHN: Some drunk or other.

LAURA: We ought to call the police.

JOHN: Don't be silly. I said it's just a drunk. It's fine. Honestly.

LAURA: Something must have happened. It sounded so sinister.

JOHN: It's in your mind, darling. That's all.

LAURA: No. I heard it.

JOHN: Laura. Don't build it up to something it isn't.

LAURA: No.

JOHN: Don't feed the imagination. That's just what you don't need.

Come on, darling. Just come with me.

LAURA: I don't want to go that way. Why won't you listen to me?

I'm going back to where the alley branched in two. Come on.

LAURA moves towards the alleyway. She leaves.

JOHN, left alone, looks around.

He sees a CHILD in a hood. We can see the red of her clothes. The CHILD is panicked and we can hear her breathing.

JOHN hesitates, wonders whether to run after her. LAURA calls out.

John.

LAURA returns.

Are you coming?

She sees JOHN staring.

What is it? Is it the scream? Has something happened?

JOHN: No. I said it was nothing.

LAURA: Oh. Well I hate to tell you, but you were wrong. We are where I thought. It's a few more streets, then there's a place. I saw it yesterday.

Come on, darling. Let's go.

JOHN looks back to where he saw the CHILD. She reappears for a second.

John. What are you looking at?

JOHN: Nothing.

LAURA: Come on, then.

JOHN: Yes. Yes of course.

JOHN follows LAURA and they leave.

RESTAURANT

The PROPRIETOR sets up for the evening.

A POLICEMAN drinks a glass of wine.

PROPRIETOR: [You want another?]

POLICEMAN: [No. I have to go.]

PROPRIETOR: [You got things to do. Glad I don't have your job.]

POLICEMAN: [No. I know.]

PROPRIETOR: [Terrible job at a time like this.]

We see the SISTERS approach the restaurant.

[Yes, glad I don't. Here come the tourists, then. My theatre opens.]

PROPRIETOR turns to SISTERS and switches on his charm.

Ladies, good evening. What can I do for you on this lovely occasion?

SISTER: Do you have a table for two?

PROPRIETOR: Certainly. Follow me.

PROPRIETOR turns to POLICEMAN, who drains his wine.

[I have to go.]

POLICEMAN: [Of course. I'll see you soon.]

PROPRIETOR: [Sure. Oh, and good luck.]

POLICEMAN: [Thanks.]

POLICEMAN leaves.

PROPRIETOR leads the SISTERS to their table, sits them down.

PROPRIETOR: And have you had a good day in our beautiful city?

SISTER: Very.

PROPRIETOR: You have seen some sights?

SISTER: We visited Torcello.

PROPRIETOR: A beautiful island.

What can I get you?

SISTER: I think a bottle of house white. And some acqua minerale. Senza gas. And the spaghetti vongole. For both of us.

PROPRIETOR: A perfect choice.

We see JOHN and LAURA arrive, LAURA leading. They are talking as they arrive and the PROPRIETOR approaches them and they don't see the SISTERS.

LAURA: You see, John. It looks lovely.

JOHN: All right.

PROPRIETOR: Good evening.

LAURA: Do you have a table for two?

PROPRIETOR: For two, lady. Of course. This way, prego.

LAURA: Thank you.

They follow the PROPRIETOR and are seated, LAURA's back to the SISTERS.

PROPRIETOR: You like this table?

LAURA: It's fine, thank you.

PROPRIETOR: My best table, only for you.

The PROPRIETOR hands them menus.

A beautiful evening in a beautiful city. And a beautiful woman.

He leaves.

LAURA: Are you happy with it so far?

JOHN: I'll reserve judgement.

LAURA: You always do when I choose.

JOHN: Does he have to be so obsequious?

LAURA: It's just an act.

They study their menus. LAURA places hers down.

JOHN: I'm dying for a drink.

JOHN calls to the PROPRIETOR.

Signore. We'll have two very large Camparis, with soda.

PROPRIETOR: Sir. And you want to order now? Or do you need longer to look?

JOHN: We shall have our drinks, then study the menu.

PROPRIETOR: Certainly. You say when you need me and I will be here immediately.

JOHN: Thank you.

PROPRIETOR leaves.

Insufferable man.

How does he know we're English? One would have thought we wore name tags.

LAURA: It's probably your manner.

JOHN: What manner?

LAURA: You know, empire, running the last outpost in
Darjeeling.

JOHN: I wish we were.

You'd be marvellous out there.

LAURA: I'd be terrible with the servants, darling. Can you
imagine?

I'd be too sympathetic.

JOHN: You have to let people know what's what.

LAURA: John.

JOHN: It's true. People like to know where they are.

LAURA laughs.

JOHN looks up, round the restaurant.

LAURA: Looking for an Italian lovely?

JOHN sees the SISTERS. Reacts.

Well?

What? What is it? She must be a real beauty for you to
look like that.

LAURA goes to turn her head.

JOHN: Laura. Did you plan for us to come here?

LAURA: You know I didn't.

JOHN: Are you sure?

LAURA: How could I have done that?

JOHN: Well you seemed pretty damned keen on dragging me
here.

LAURA: John? What a peculiar thing to say. What is the matter
with you?

JOHN: Nothing. It's just I'm not sure I can bear that waiter.

PROPRIETOR brings drinks.

LAURA: Thank you so much.

JOHN ignores the PROPRIETOR. Picks up the glass and drinks.

(*Chastising.*) John.

LAURA holds her glass up to touch them.

JOHN: Sorry.

They touch glasses.

LAURA: To a lovely day.

JOHN: Yes. Of course. A lovely day.

LAURA picks up her menu and studies it quickly, places it down, drinks, then goes to look around.

LAURA: So where's this beauty you were eyeing?

JOHN: (*Quick.*) Tomorrow, we need to talk about tomorrow.

LAURA: Oh. What about it?

JOHN: I was thinking we should get the car out, do that drive to Padua.

LAURA: We could.

JOHN: There's the cathedral and the Giotto frescos, and the villas along the Brenta.

LAURA: I don't know. I don't feel right now I could even see another cathedral. Let's decide at breakfast.

Now, who can be here? Any likely candidates?

LAURA begins to look around, sees the SISTERS.

Good grief. How extraordinary. How truly amazing.

JOHN: What?

LAURA: Look, John. There they are. My wonderful old twins. And they've seen us.

40

LAURA waves. The SISTER smiles and bows.

Is that why you asked if I had planned for us to come here?

It is, isn't it?

JOHN: Well it does seem an extraordinary coincidence. We go to Torcello and they're there. Now we are back in Venice they crop up here.

Do you know how many restaurants there are in Venice?

LAURA: Well it is a coincidence. Nothing more. Nothing sinister.

Oh, darling. I must go and speak to them. I must tell them how happy I've been all day, thanks to them and their vision. If the waiter comes, get me some scampi.

JOHN: Oh for heaven's sake.

LAURA: Don't be like that. I won't be a moment.

LAURA walks to the SISTERS, sits with them.

JOHN bolts his drink and calls the PROPRIETOR over.

JOHN: Another the same.

PROPRIETOR: And to eat? Or you would like another Campari to eat? (*Laughs.*)

JOHN: (*Cold.*) I don't think so. Do you?

JOHN looks at the menu quickly.

I'll have the veal.

PROPRIETOR: This one, sir?

JOHN: This one, yes.

PROPRIETOR: A very good choice. And for the lady?

JOHN: Scampi. Nothing more. And a bottle of soave, with ice.

PROPRIETOR: Sorry, sir. In place of the Campari?

JOHN: No. I'd like both, now. Please.

PROPRIETOR: Yes, sir. What you like, sir.

Thank you.

PROPRIETOR leaves.

JOHN: Prego bloody prego.

JOHN takes Laura's drink and bolts it. He watches LAURA and the SISTERS.

PROPRIETOR leaves. JOHN stares at SISTERS and LAURA.

PROPRIETOR brings a tray. Gives JOHN his Campari. JOHN hands him his empty glass.

PROPRIETOR: I think you enjoyed that.

JOHN ignores him.

PROPRIETOR goes to pour the wine.

JOHN: Please. Leave it there.

PROPRIETOR: You have no need to taste it?

JOHN: No. It's fine.

PROPRIETOR: Sir.

JOHN: Tell the Signora. (*Points at LAURA.*) Her drink is here.

PROPRIETOR: Sir.

PROPRIETOR moves to the table, speaks to LAURA, who looks over, as do the SISTERS.

PROPRIETOR returns with an accordion and approaches JOHN. JOHN looks away. The PROPRIETOR begins to play.

JOHN: I'm sorry. Please, no music.

PROPRIETOR: No music?

JOHN: No. I'm sorry. I was enjoying the quiet.

PROPRIETOR: I can play more quietly.

JOHN: I'd rather just be left alone.

PROPRIETOR: Of course.

JOHN finishes the next Campari. He holds his head, then walks over. Stands at their table.

LAURA: (*To SISTERS.*) This is my husband, John.

JOHN: Good evening.

Laura. Your drink is there.

LAURA: Yes. The waiter said.

JOHN: I think you should come back over to our table.

LAURA: John. Please don't be rude.

JOHN: I'm not being rude.

Look, my wife is very tired. She really needs some peace.

LAURA: John. I'm fine.

There's something I want you to hear.

JOHN: I was afraid there might be.

SISTER: Please. May I speak?

My sister has had another vision.

JOHN: (*Laughs.*) I had a feeling you might say that. Go on, what is it? I suppose you're going to tell us that Christine is here with us, even though it would be well past her bedtime?

SISTER: My sister says you are in danger if you stay in Venice.

Long silence.

LAURA: John. Why don't you say something?

SISTER: My sister says as long as you leave tomorrow, you will be fine.

JOHN: Are you really telling me we should leave Venice?

SISTER: Yes. It was your daughter who told her.

JOHN: Oh, for God's sake.

LAURA: Please, John. Don't be rude.

JOHN: Rude? I'd say sabotaging our holiday is pretty rude.

SISTER: Sabotage is not a word I would use.

JOHN: I am sure you wouldn't.

SISTER: Let me explain.

JOHN: Go on. Fire away.

SISTER: Please. I am asking you to listen.

> We have studied the occult all our lives. But since my sister went blind, these visions have really taken hold.
>
> It is as though her sight were driven right inside her, and she were able to access new things. Things people do not know. It is as though losing the one sense has developed another.

JOHN: Yes, yes.

SISTER: Please. Allow me to finish.

> You see, there are things we do not know. There are sounds we can not hear. Colours we can not see. Early signs of earthquakes and fits that animals can sense but we can not.
>
> Human beings think they know everything, but there is so much more out there than we can see and feel.

JOHN: Have you finished?

SISTER: No. I want you to understand this has some rational, scientific basis.

JOHN: I am sure you do. However, my real concern is my wife. She really does not need to be listening to any of this bloody nonsense.

> Darling, come on. You've heard enough.

BLIND SISTER: Don't go.

JOHN: What do you want me to do? Stay here in this, this
– cabal? And solemnly believe every word?

I'm afraid we have a holiday to continue.

BLIND SISTER: No.

You are in danger. Did you hear me? If you stay in Venice
you are in danger.

JOHN: Oh. Am I?

LAURA: John. Please.

BLIND SISTER: You are closing your mind. Locking the gates.

BLIND SISTER reaches out, feels for JOHN's arm.

But you can see.

You can truly see.

SISTER: My dear, that's enough.

BLIND SISTER: No.

There are vibrations. Understandings.

You are en rapport with the unknown.

You are psychic.

JOHN laughs.

JOHN: Well this is marvellous.

LAURA: John.

JOHN: No.

Let's make sure we have it straight. First I'm to believe I'm
in danger if I stay here in Venice. Yes?

BLIND SISTER: Yes.

JOHN: Second I'm to believe that I'm psychic.

BLIND SISTER: Yes. You have real sight.

JOHN: Wonderful.

So it's my psychic intuition telling me I don't have to listen to any more of this nonsense.

In fact it is telling me I need to get my poor wife the hell out of here. You see, I think she has had enough to deal with without all this, don't you?

Laura. Come on.

JOHN stands.

Come on, Laura. Now.

JOHN walks back to his table.

LAURA: I'm sorry. I'm so sorry.

SISTER: We do understand.

We really do.

LAURA returns to the table.

PROPRIETOR approaches with bread. JOHN puts his hand up. PROPRIETOR hesitates, backs away during following.

LAURA: John.

JOHN: No.

LAURA: I think we should listen.

JOHN: No. I can not stay here a moment longer.

And I can't allow you to.

JOHN takes bills from his pocket, places them on the table.

Come on.

JOHN goes to leave. LAURA looks over at the SISTERS.

JOHN looks back.

Laura. Come on.

LAURA leaves to catch up with JOHN. The PROPRIETOR takes away their plates of food.

The SISTERS eat, and we see JOHN and LAURA are:

OUTSIDE

There is a light rain and JOHN and LAURA are wet.

LAURA: John, please listen.

JOHN ignores her.

John.

Listen to me.

JOHN: No. I think I've listened enough this evening.

LAURA: Oh, John.

JOHN: (*Looking round.*) I hate this bloody city. The stink of slimy water.

LAURA: Don't say that.

JOHN: You can feel it sinking. One day it'll all have gone. All this deep down under the water.

LAURA: Don't say that.

Venice hasn't changed. It's the same beautiful place.

JOHN: Is it? (*Laughs.*) Is it?

It doesn't look the same now. Shuttered windows. The water, black as oil.

And the gondolas lined up like, like bloody coffins.

LAURA: John, stop it.

JOHN: What?

LAURA: You know what.

Look, we have to talk about what the sisters said.

JOHN: Do we?

LAURA: Of course we do. We can't just ignore it.

JOHN: Actually I think we can. We can absolutely ignore it.

LAURA: Oh, John. You drank too much on an empty stomach. You know it goes to your head. You can't think rationally.

JOHN: So now it's you telling me to think rationally. Really, darling. That is pathetic.

LAURA: You were overreacting, running off like that.

JOHN laughs.

JOHN: Was I indeed?

LAURA: What will they think?

JOHN: I really don't care. In fact I couldn't care less.

LAURA: John.

Oh, for heaven's sake.

JOHN: There's no 'oh, for heaven's sake'. What is it you want exactly? You want to believe them? You really do?

LAURA: I think we should take it seriously.

JOHN: Oh do you. In that case, do you want me to go straight back to the hotel? I could tell your friend the clerk we're planning to leave first thing. Sorry for the inconvenience I'll say. Yes we were having a lovely holiday in your beautiful city, in your lovely hotel where you look after us so well, but unfortunately we met two strangers and they ordered us to go.

Yes, I'll say, I know it sounds odd, to be told to end a holiday by strangers, but you know how it is. These things happen.

Waits.

You see how bloody absurd it sounds?

LAURA: Why are you being like this?

JOHN: You know why? Because I am wet and cross. In a wet city which is sinking. Laura, I'm just not in a mood to discuss this.

LAURA: Oh, John, and the day was going so well.

JOHN: It wasn't me who ruined it. It was your nonsense. Your weird sisters.

LAURA: They are not weird.

You know, I had such hope after today. I felt I could see some light at the end, but now I feel back to the worst of it.

JOHN: That's what I was trying to say. It's not good for you to listen.

LAURA: I just feel I'm back to seeing her in your arms and her bare feet hanging down.

JOHN: Stop it. Please stop it.

LAURA: I'm just back to that and us helpless to do anything.

JOHN: Hang on. Are you trying to say something? Are you saying it was me who couldn't save her.

LAURA: Oh, God, no.

JOHN: Because neither of us could, if you remember.

LAURA: I'm not saying that.

JOHN: Neither of us, Laura.

LAURA: John, please. I'm not saying that.

JOHN: Well it's beginning to sound like it.

LAURA: I don't mean it like that. You know I don't. It's just the booze making you think like that.

JOHN: Oh is it?

LAURA: Yes, darling. Look you know I don't think that. Don't you?

JOHN: I suppose.

Pause.

LAURA: John. Don't be cross if I say something.

JOHN: Go on.

LAURA: It's just that if we stay in Venice, I shall have a nasty, nagging feeling inside. I'll keep thinking of Christine being unhappy and be worried for your safety and wanting us to go. I do think we should leave.

49

JOHN: Do you?

LAURA: I do, yes.

JOHN: Look, darling. Christine can't be worried or unhappy.

Christine is dead.

LAURA: Oh, John. Don't say that.

JOHN: No.

LAURA: Please don't say that. Not that.

Pause.

JOHN: Oh, God.

I'm sorry. I'm so sorry.

Pause.

JOHN holds LAURA's arms, scrutinises her face.

Sometimes, darling, you look just like her.

LAURA: Do I?

JOHN: Yes.

Here. (*Touches.*) Between your eyebrows. This little line.
When you frown. It's exactly the same.

LAURA: Oh, John.

JOHN: Laura.

They embrace. JOHN holds her arms.

Are you all right?

LAURA: I think so.

JOHN: I don't want you to think about what the sisters said.

LAURA turns away.

Look, darling, I don't think they're quite balanced.

LAURA: That's so unfair, John. They are genuine, I know it.

JOHN: How?

LAURA: They're so sincere.

JOHN: I agree they seem sincere, but that doesn't make them well balanced.

LAURA: I knew you would take it like this. I told them you would.

JOHN: Laura. I want you to listen.

However many times she tells you otherwise, I am not psychic. I am not 'en rapport with the unknown'.

There is nothing out there we can not see.

There is nothing out there we do not know.

There is only the here and now.

Understood?

Yes or no?

No response.

Laura?

Laura?

LAURA: The thing is, John, you can't force me to see things the way you do.

Whatever you say I shall think what I think and you think what you think.

No response.

Oh, John. Let's go back to the hotel.

Come on.

LAURA takes JOHN's hand and they leave.

HOTEL

A POLICEMAN leans on the desk.

CLERK: [Any news?]

POLICEMAN: [Yes. Finally. There's a pattern to it all. They're happening near here. My men are everywhere.]

CLERK: [Will you get him?]

POLICEMAN: [Yes.]

[God willing, your tourists will be safe.]

JOHN and LAURA approach.

The CLERK waves at JOHN, gets key and envelope.

CLERK: This came for you.

POLICEMAN: [I'd better go. I'll see you soon.]

CLERK: [Good night.]

(*To JOHN.*) Here.

POLICEMAN leaves.

JOHN: (*Taking key.*) Can I have some black coffee sent to our room.

LAURA: John. Let's have it down here.

JOHN: I need to dry off.

CLERK: Sir, this came for you.

LAURA: (*To CLERK.*) What is it?

JOHN: Come on, Laura. Let's go.

JOHN moves away.

LAURA takes the telegram. The CLERK then leaves.

LAURA: John. What can it be?

JOHN: What?

LAURA: This. A telegram.

LAURA holds up the telegram.

What is it?

JOHN softens, approaches.

JOHN: Let me.

JOHN takes the telegram, opens it, reads.

It's from Mr Hill. It's Johnnie.

JOHN sees LAURA's reaction.

It's all right. He's in hospital with suspected appendicitis. The surgeon says there's no cause for alarm.

LAURA: Oh, John.

JOHN: Just suspected, that's all. It might be nothing.

Look, he's in the right place. And anyway things may have changed. He could be fine, back at school in the san.

LAURA: John.

JOHN: Oh, Laura. It'll be all right.

LAURA: But this decides it, doesn't it? Here is the proof.

JOHN: Darling, it's not proof. This is just a coincidence.

Johnnie being ill is just something that happened.

We could have got this telegram any time.

LAURA: No.

John. We have to leave Venice tomorrow because we're going home.

Can't you see? It's Johnnie who's in danger, not you.

This is what Christine was trying to tell the twins.

LAURA walks away, leaves JOHN alone.

We see the BLIND SISTER staring at him.

We hear the scream from earlier.

Lights down.

Act Two

Morning, and we are in:

HOTEL BEDROOM

LAURA has started packing. JOHN picks up the telephone. He checks the telegram.

JOHN: Can you put me through to the international operator. Thank you.

Great Britain.

Hampstead 6362.

It is urgent. Thank you.

He replaces the receiver.

LAURA: Whatever the news, I am going back.

JOHN: Look, darling, just wait and see. I'm sure they'll say he's fine and the scare is over.

LAURA: No. I am going today. Whatever flight they manage to get for me.

JOHN: Wait and see. I'm sure we can drive back together. Surely a day or so won't make a difference.

LAURA: It might not to you, but it does to me. I've already lost one child, John. I'm not going to lose another.

JOHN: No. No. Of course.

Pause as they both think about Laura's words.

Then LAURA continues to pack and JOHN watches. Then,

Look, if you're really going to fly back, shouldn't I come with you?

LAURA: What about the car? And all this.

JOHN: I could come back for the car when Johnnie's better.

LAURA: There's no need. It would cost a fortune.

JOHN: I suppose.

LAURA: Anyway as long as I get there in time. That's what's important.

LAURA picks up the phone to check it is working. Replaces it.

(*To phone.*) Come on. Come on.

LAURA continues packing.

Close this one for me, darling.

JOHN closes the case.

How are you going to get all this in?

JOHN: I'll have your empty seat.

LAURA: Of course. Stupid of me.

JOHN: I'm not looking forward to going back on my own.

LAURA: By the time you're sorted here and get to Milan, the day'll be over.

JOHN: Then a night on the train on my own. And the ferry from Calais.

LAURA: You're beginning to sound more concerned about coming back on your own, than you are about Johnnie.

JOHN: That's not fair.

LAURA: It's how you sound.

JOHN: It's not what I meant.

LAURA: Then how am I supposed to know what you mean? You always do this. You say something so different from what you mean.

JOHN: I don't.

LAURA: You do.

You keep what you really think inside. All in there. (*Points at her chest.*)

JOHN: I'm a man.

LAURA: I did notice.

> But you could still tell me what you feel. It's as though I pour everything out and get nothing back.

JOHN: Laura, you really should calm down.

LAURA: Will you please stop telling me to calm down.

JOHN: You're getting terribly agitated.

LAURA: Am I? It's not surprising really, is it?

JOHN: I suppose not.

LAURA: Suppose?

JOHN: Stop interrogating my every word.

LAURA: I'm not interrogating you.

> I just wish you'd tell me what you feel.

JOHN: Do you?

LAURA: Yes I really do.

JOHN: Then what I suggest is, you use this. (*Points at head.*) Then work out what I feel.

LAURA: What do you mean?

JOHN: What do you think I mean?

> Look, Laura, you're not the only one to suffer. Sometimes it's as though you're wearing the crown and I'm not allowed to feel.

LAURA: That's a terrible thing to say.

JOHN: I know, but it's true.

LAURA: How can you say that?

JOHN: You made me. Look, it's impossible. If I say nothing it's not good enough. So I say what I feel and that isn't either.

> You see, I feel as deeply as you.

Pause.

My job as a man is to protect my family. That is you and my children. And I couldn't.

I couldn't save her, and I can't save you from all of this.

So in addition to everything, I am left with an overriding sense of my failure as a man.

That is what I feel.

But neither of us feel any better that I have said it.

LAURA: Oh God.

I'm sorry. John. I'm so sorry.

JOHN: It doesn't matter.

LAURA: It does. We have to stop this. We mustn't fight over this any more.

JOHN: No.

Come here.

JOHN embraces LAURA. They hold each other for a while. Then LAURA breaks away.

LAURA: I must get this done.

LAURA busies herself packing.

JOHN watches, then goes to bathroom to collect more things. The phone rings and JOHN rushes to answer it, but LAURA gets there first.

Yes, speaking. (*Pause.*) Hello, Mr Hill. Yes, of course.

I see. At what time? What's that?

Oh dear, are you sure?

I see.

Yes.

JOHN goes to take the phone. LAURA gestures for him to let her continue.

Well I will be there as soon as possible. I'm hoping to be on the early afternoon flight, so I'll be there by seven at the very latest, unless there's a delay.

Be sure to tell him, won't you? And do send him our love.

Thank you, yes. Thank you.

Puts phone down.

They are going to operate today.

JOHN: Oh, darling.

You mustn't worry. He'll be absolutely fine. It's routine. They do them all the time.

LAURA: The surgeon said it's slightly awkward in his case. The X-ray shows the appendix is in a tricky position.

JOHN: What does he mean?

LAURA: That's all he said.

JOHN: You should have let me speak.

LAURA suddenly sits down.

Laura?

LAURA: I should be there.

JOHN: You will be.

LAURA: I should be there now.

Pause. JOHN tries to hold LAURA but she pushes him away.

I actually can't bear this.

JOHN: No.

LAURA: I just can not bear it.

JOHN: Laura.

LAURA: No.

JOHN stands, at a loss.

You see, whatever anyone says, nothing will make me feel better. This has happened to me, I have lost my daughter. And my son is having an operation, they are putting him to sleep and cutting him open, and I am not there when he needs me the most.

This is truly unbearable.

LAURA sits, stunned.

Knock on the door, the CLERK enters.

JOHN: Yes.

CLERK: Excuse me, sir, signora.

He sees LAURA.

I'm sorry.

JOHN: It's all right. The bags aren't ready yet. I'll call when they are.

CLERK: It's not the bags.

LAURA stands up, panicked.

LAURA: Has someone rung?

CLERK: No. No. A ticket has become available on a charter flight which leaves soon.

LAURA: Oh God. I thought you were going to say something else.

So I can go this morning?

JOHN: Hold on, Laura.

LAURA: No, darling. Look, that's wonderful. Thank you.

JOHN: But Laura.

LAURA: I know what I'm doing. What time is the flight?

CLERK: The group is leaving the hotel in five minutes. If you are in the reception, you can go with them.

LAURA: I'll be there. Tell them that, won't you? One minute and I'll be down. Tell them.

Thank you. Thank you so much.

CLERK: Signora. I will tell them.

CLERK leaves. LAURA immediately begins sorting what she needs.

JOHN: Laura.

LAURA: Don't try to stop me. It's all working out.

JOHN: But are you sure you want to do this? Charters can be so unreliable.

LAURA: Oh, John. I could be there when he comes round, don't you see? I can be there to hold his hand. Like I ought to be.

LAURA gets her handbag.

I don't need any of this stuff. Just passport and money.

JOHN takes out some notes, hands them over.

JOHN: Here. Take this. And this. I can always cash some more travellers' cheques if I need to.

LAURA: Thank you. Oh, what a relief.

You will call tonight, won't you? When you get to Milan. And don't make that face. You'll be in Calais in the morning, then it'll be just the hop over the water.

You've got Mr Hill's number? They said I could stay there tonight.

JOHN: Yes.

LAURA: Right, that has to be everything.

JOHN: You're quite a whirlwind.

LAURA: A whirlwind?

I'm a mother, John.

You will call tonight?

JOHN: Of course I will.

LAURA: God. Five minutes, he said.

Hold me, darling.

JOHN embraces LAURA. He lets go.

LAURA puts on her green coat. Picks up her bag. Kisses JOHN.

Don't forget to call, and... (*Looking around.*) ...I'm sorry to leave you with all this.

JOHN: It's fine.

Are you all right, darling?

LAURA nods, but she isn't.

Oh, darling.

JOHN embraces her again, then LAURA pushes away.

LAURA: I have to go.

JOHN: Let me come down with you.

LAURA: No.

I'm better alone, I can get a grip.

JOHN: Sure.

LAURA nods, composes herself.

Ready?

LAURA: Yes.

I'll speak to you tonight. Think of me.

JOHN: Of course I will.

LAURA: And drive carefully.

LAURA kisses him again and then leaves.

Silence.

JOHN stands in the room, alone. He turns back to the packing and fingers Laura's clothes, folds them, closes the case. He looks at the headscarves he bought her, then picks up her dress. He smells it and holds it to his face, lowers his head.

A knock at the door. JOHN doesn't hear it. Another knock.

JOHN: Come in.

The CLERK enters cautiously.

CLERK: Sir.

You didn't hear me?

JOHN: No. No. I was just –

CLERK: Sorry.

JOHN: No, no. It's fine.

CLERK: I came to tell you your wife, she has gone.

JOHN: Good. Thank you.

CLERK: She'll be in England soon.

JOHN: Yes.

CLERK: Sir. Are these cases ready?

JOHN: This one is, yes.

Thank you for organising the flight.

CLERK: My pleasure.

JOHN: I'm sorry we're leaving so abruptly.

CLERK: It's not easy to leave Venice.

JOHN: No.

It always feels like leaving another world. It does
something to the imagination, I feel. Lights a fire inside.

CLERK: That's a beautiful thing to say.

JOHN: Oh. Oh. Thank you.

JOHN stands and closes another case.

I'll take the direct vaporetto to Piazzale Roma for the car.

CLERK takes another case out. We hear a siren.

Tell me, what is going on out there?

CLERK: What?

JOHN: All the police. It wasn't like this when we were last here.

CLERK: No.

JOHN: So what is going on?

CLERK: It won't affect you now you are leaving Venice. There have been some deaths.

JOHN: What do you mean? What deaths?

CLERK: Some murders.

JOHN: Murders? I haven't heard anything.

CLERK: They tried to keep it quiet.

JOHN: Why?

CLERK: They were tourists.

JOHN: I see.

CLERK: One was discovered only last night. A man this time. A woman last week. Their throats had been cut.

JOHN: Perfectly ghastly.

CLERK: Yes. We worry about the tourists. Without them, there is nothing.

JOHN: Do they know who is doing it?

CLERK: They say they are getting nearer to finding out.

It should soon be over.

JOHN: That's a relief.

CLERK: Anyway, as I say, it won't affect you now you are leaving Venice.

Is that bag ready?

JOHN: No. I'll bring that one. It's not heavy.

CLERK: Is there anything else I can do for you?

JOHN: No. Thank you.

Look, I wanted to say, you've been most helpful while we've been here. I'd like to give you this.

JOHN gives him a large tip.

CLERK: Thank you. But it is my pleasure.

Sir. I am very sorry about your son.

JOHN: Thank you. I am sure he'll be fine. It's his appendix. (*Points.*) Here.

CLERK: *Appendice.*

JOHN: It's a common problem. Routine.

But everything to do with children is a worry.

You worry when they are babies, and then they get older and you think you will worry less, but you don't.

There's no end to it.

CLERK: No.

Your wife, she is a lovely woman.

JOHN: Yes. Yes she is, isn't she?

CLERK goes to leave.

You know.

She wouldn't have said, but –

CLERK turns.

You see we came here on our honeymoon ten years ago. We came back because – we lost our daughter recently. She was ill, meningitis. We drove her to hospital, but it was too late.

She was a young girl, dark hair. She could have passed as an Italian. Every time I see a child here...

Christine, her name was. Christine.

CLERK: I am so sorry.

JOHN: It's the most terrible thing.

CLERK: I really am sorry.

JOHN: (*Realises.*) Oh God. I shouldn't have said. With your wife being pregnant. Stupid of me.

CLERK: No. Not at all.

JOHN: It wasn't a normal thing to happen. And it's rare. Your child will be fine.

I'm sorry.

CLERK: It is different. They are two different things.

JOHN: Yes. Yes. Of course.

Thank you.

CLERK: Is there anything else?

JOHN: No. But tell me, what is that music?

CLERK: What music?

JOHN: Outside the window.

CLERK: Something for tourists. But it is very quiet. I can only just hear it.

JOHN: I see. It keeps getting louder.

CLERK: Are you all right, sir?

JOHN: All right? Yes, of course.

CLERK: You can manage now?

JOHN: I'm absolutely fine.

Sorry. You had to listen to my nonsense.

CLERK: It's not nonsense, no.

JOHN: Right. Well good luck with it all and thank you again.

CLERK: Not at all, sir. Goodbye.

JOHN doesn't respond.

CLERK leaves.

JOHN is alone with his cases, in the:

VENICE STREET

JOHN lights a cigarette and looks around.

We see LAURA and the SISTERS enter. LAURA wears her green coat and is distressed. The SISTER has an arm around her shoulder. BLIND SISTER holds her arm.

JOHN stares, fixed. He moves, calls out:

JOHN: Laura. Laura.

But she can not hear him. They pass and leave.

JOHN attempts to follow, but his way is blocked by a MUSICIAN.

Out of my way. God's sake.

MUSICIAN: [You get out of my way.]

[A person can't even walk in his own city.]

MUSICIAN leaves.

JOHN is alone. He looks in the direction where he saw LAURA.

CLERK appears.

CLERK: Sir. Your room key. I forgot to get your key.

JOHN: Where is she?

CLERK: Who?

JOHN: My wife.

CLERK: I'm sorry, sir.

JOHN: I've just seen my wife.

CLERK: No. I saw her leave myself. To the airport with the group.

JOHN: She was just here.

CLERK: It can't be your wife.

JOHN: It was. I know it was. She wore her green coat, and she was with these two ladies we met. Two sisters. Identical twins. The three of them together.

CLERK: I don't understand.

JOHN: There must be some explanation.

(*Working it out.*) Perhaps the flight was delayed. Perhaps she thought to come back and catch me before I left.

CLERK: The airport is a long way.

JOHN: Yes. So why would she do that?

CLERK: Maybe she changed her mind? Decided to not go back?

JOHN: No. She was desperate to get back.

They both think.

CLERK: She was with two friends?

JOHN: Two ladies, yes. The sisters.

CLERK: Then she went with them to their hotel?

JOHN: We don't know where they are staying. We only met them yesterday.

But anyway why would she have gone anywhere with them?

CLERK: Would you like me to telephone the airport and see if the flight left?

JOHN: Of course. Yes. Thank you.

CLERK leaves. We hear his voice offstage, in Italian.

JOHN stands alone, waits.

CLERK: (*Offstage.*) [Can I check a flight? Charter to London.]

[To London, yes? It departed. No problems?]

[And you had no passengers go missing?]

[Thank you.]

[Yes. Good day.]

CLERK returns.

JOHN: What did they say?

CLERK: The flight left at the correct time. No problems.

Is it possible you made a mistake?

JOHN: No. I'm absolutely certain.

JOHN paces.

This is ridiculous. What on earth can have happened?

CLERK: I don't know what to suggest.

JOHN: No. Well I can't just wait here. I'll go and see if I can find out where those damned sisters are staying.

CLERK: Sir.

JOHN: But if she comes here, don't let her go and look for me. Or we'll be chasing each other through the streets all night. You understand?

Tell her I will not leave Venice without her.

CLERK leaves and JOHN is alone. He smokes and thinks. JOHN moves and is in:

RESTAURANT

JOHN approaches the PROPRIETOR.

JOHN: Excuse me. Excuse me.

I'm sorry to bother you. I don't know if you remember, but I was here last night.

I came with my wife.

You must remember me.

Something happened and we had to leave suddenly.

No response.

It was last night.

PROPRIETOR: You left without eating your food.

68

JOHN: I am so sorry. It was my wife, she became upset.

PROPRIETOR: Did she?

JOHN: She did, yes.

> Look, I have a real problem. My wife is missing. I mean I saw her earlier and now I can not find her.

PROPRIETOR: She isn't here.

JOHN: No. I know, I mean I can see. But you see she was with the sisters when I saw her.

PROPRIETOR: What sisters?

PROPRIETOR goes to turn away.

JOHN: Please.

> Look I do apologise for last night. I mean sincerely.

> I am beginning to worry, you understand. I thought perhaps you had seen the sisters again. The twins.

PROPRIETOR: Twins?

JOHN: Due. Gemelle. One of them was blind.

JOHN covers his eye.

PROPRIETOR: Ah. Gemelli. Gemelli dello specchio.

JOHN: I need to find them urgently.

> Do you know where they are staying?

PROPRIETOR: No.

> Perhaps you should come back tonight, sir, in case they are here. Perhaps this time you could stay and eat your food.

JOHN: I said I am sorry.

> I need to find her.

PROPRIETOR: Why? Do you think she is in danger?

JOHN: Danger?

PROPRIETOR: Another tourist has been murdered.

JOHN: No.

PROPRIETOR: Here.

(*Points to throat.*) Just here.

JOHN: No.

Don't do that. Please don't say that.

PROPRIETOR: The canals are full of blood.

JOHN: What on earth are you saying, man?

PROPRIETOR: Saying? I am saying nothing. I say in Venice the whole world meets. She will come to you.

JOHN: I thought you said something else.

How very odd. I am sorry.

JOHN is alone again. He hears a CHILD's laughter. Stops. Listens.

A MUSICIAN enters and begins to play.

JOHN approaches.

Excuse me.

MUSICIAN: Sir, you name a song, I play it.

JOHN: No song, no.

I am looking for a woman.

MUSICIAN: We are all looking for a woman. All men all over the world look for women.

JOHN: You don't understand.

MUSICIAN: But I do understand. I understand exactly.

JOHN: I have lost my wife.

She's very distinctive. She is wearing a green coat.

MUSICIAN: Tell me, is she beautiful?

JOHN: Beautiful, yes.

MUSICIAN: And she wears a green coat?

JOHN: Yes. And she is with two ladies. Twins. One is blind.

MUSICIAN: A blind twin?

JOHN: Yes. Where did you see her?

MUSICIAN: I haven't.

JOHN: Oh.

MUSICIAN: But I may see her.

JOHN: Please, if you do, tell her I will be at the hotel.

MUSICIAN: I will look for them.

But first I must play you a song.

JOHN: No.

MUSICIAN: But I have to play for you. For my money. You see, I have children to feed. Mouths to fill. Yes, sir. Mouths to fill.

MUSICIAN begins to play for JOHN.

JOHN: No.

I have to find her.

Anything could be happening to her.

MUSICIAN stops playing.

MUSICIAN: Was she sizing up her neck?

JOHN: What?

MUSICIAN: The blind sister, was she sizing up her neck?

A string of pearls like drops of blood.

JOHN: Why do you say that?

MUSICIAN goes to leave.

Don't go.

Why did you say that?

Please help me. Please.

MUSICIAN plays as he leaves.

JOHN remains, alone. He sees the shadow of a CHILD.

Then JOHN hears Christine's voice calling.

VOICE: Daddy, daddy.

JOHN whips round, shocked, calls out.

JOHN: Christine.

A WAITER enters, played by the CLERK.

WAITER: Sir. Sir. You want something to drink. Coffee? Chocolate?

JOHN: No thank you.

I'm looking for someone.

WAITER: In Venice? A good joke, yes.

JOHN: Not a joke. I really am.

WAITER: Look I'm busy. Okay?

WAITER goes to leave.

JOHN: I'm looking for my wife. She is with these two women.

She's a tourist.

WAITER: Do you know how many tourists there are here?

JOHN: But she looks so distinctive.

WAITER: No tourist is distinctive. Believe me.

JOHN: The women are twins. Identical twins. One is blind. Freaks.

WAITER: How interesting.

Look, I'm busy. Do you want a drink?

JOHN: No.

Please think if you have seen her.

WAITER: I don't have time to think. I have people to serve, money to be earned.

WAITER goes to leave.

JOHN: You look like someone.

WAITER: Do I?

Are you all right, sir?

JOHN: I think so.

WAITER: You can sit here. That's it. Sit there and place your head down. You look faint.

JOHN sits. WAITER pushes his head down to his knees.

The WAITER bends down and talks right into JOHN's ear.

Don't look now.

I said don't look now, but have you seen the child?

JOHN: What?

JOHN looks round.

WAITER: Don't be too obvious, darling.

JOHN: What are you saying? What child?

WAITER: I'm sorry, sir? What is it you are saying?

JOHN: You said don't look now. You said have I seen the child.

WAITER: No, sir. I said do you want something to eat?

JOHN: Eat?

WAITER: Yes, eat sir.

JOHN: Is that what you said?

WAITER: I did.

JOHN: I'm sorry.

I'm sorry.

WAITER: Well?

JOHN: What?

WAITER: Do you need anything to eat?

JOHN: No.

Do you need a glass of water?

JOHN: What?

WAITER: I said what is below the water?

JOHN stares.

Sir.

A glass of water?

JOHN: Yes. Yes please.

WAITER: Tuck your head in. There right between the knees. I'll get your water.

Stay here and she will come to you. The whole world comes to Venice.

WAITER leaves.

JOHN hears Christine's voice.

VOICE: No. No.

Daddy. Help me.

JOHN spins round again, tried to see where the voice has come from.

WAITER returns with a glass of water, but this time he is played by the PROPRIETOR.

WAITER: Here.

JOHN: What are you doing here?

WAITER: You do look faint, sir. Drink this.

WAITER pushes JOHN's head down.

JOHN hears Christine's voice whispering.

VOICE: Daddy. Daddy. Please.

JOHN: Did you hear that?

WAITER: Hear what?

JOHN: That.

WAITER: There is nothing there, sir.

JOHN: Who are you?

I don't understand. Why are you here?

WAITER: Do you want anything else? A coffee? A chocolate? Or something stronger?

JOHN: No.

WAITER: It is not easy to leave Venice, sir.

JOHN: What are you saying?

WAITER: It always feels like leaving another world. It does something to the imagination, I feel. Lights a fire inside.

JOHN: Please stop.

WAITER: Sir. I asked if you want a brandy. You really do look faint.

Pause.

JOHN: My wife.

Anything could have happened to her. She could be in danger.

JOHN touches his throat.

Her skin. Her throat.

JOHN tries to stand, begins to fall. WAITER holds him.

WAITER: What was the weight of the child's body in your arms? Was it a dead weight, sir?

A dead weight.

You couldn't save her, could you?

What about this one?

Can you save this one?

JOHN: (*Shouts.*) Sick. I am sick.

WAITER hands JOHN the water and he drinks, then the water spills from his mouth.

I can not take any more.

I can not take any more.

POLICE STATION

JOHN: Two sisters. Freaks.

Two. Due. Gemelle.

POLICE CHIEF waits.

Two identical twins.

Diabolical.

Freaks who have a hold. Their arms around her.

A dreadful hold on my wife.

Some criminal intent.

Pause. POLICE CHIEF waits.

The twins. A couple of freaks.

They could be jewel thieves.

Murderers.

I know about the murders.

POLICE CHIEF: Murders, sir?

JOHN: Yes.

Since we first saw them…

They have followed us, caused so many problems.

POLICE CHIEF: Who?

JOHN: The sisters.

Criminal designs upon my wife.

My wife...

POLICE CHIEF: Yes, your wife.

JOHN: She is missing.

POLICE CHIEF: I know. My men have given me your statement.

JOHN: Then you must understand, I am so worried.

I am beside myself with worry.

POLICE CHIEF: Of course.

JOHN: Beside myself.

POLICE CHIEF: Then perhaps you need a moment.

POLICE CHIEF leaves JOHN alone for a moment, then returns.

How do you know about the murders?

JOHN: What? Oh, that. There are police everywhere.

POLICE CHIEF waits.

And I overheard something at the hotel.

POLICE CHIEF writes a note.

POLICE CHIEF: Tell me, why did you make a connection between all this and the murders?

JOHN: Did I?

POLICE CHIEF: You did, yes.

JOHN: You understand, it is such an odd thing.

POLICE CHIEF: What is?

JOHN: All of this. Seeing my wife. With those women. Not knowing where she is.

POLICE CHIEF: And you are sure it was your wife you saw?

JOHN: Positive. Absolutely positive.

POLICE CHIEF picks up statement, checks something.

POLICE CHIEF: Where exactly did you say you saw her?

JOHN: Near the hotel.

POLICE CHIEF: Which street?

JOHN: I don't know. I don't remember the name of it.

POLICE CHIEF: No?

What time was it?

JOHN: I really don't know. Around lunchtime.

POLICE CHIEF: I see.

POLICE CHIEF waits.

Had there been arguments between you?

JOHN: No. I mean yes.

POLICE CHIEF: What kind of arguments?

JOHN: Not arguments, no. I mean just tensions. You know.

POLICE CHIEF: Tensions?

JOHN: We have been under great strain.

Anyway what relevance does that have?

POLICE CHIEF: What kind of strain?

JOHN: It says in there. We lost our daughter.

POLICE CHIEF: So tensions. Any real differences of opinion between you?

JOHN: What on earth has this got to do with it?

POLICE CHIEF: Sir?

JOHN: What exactly are you trying to insinuate?

POLICE CHIEF: Insinuate? I am not insinuating anything.

POLICE CHIEF begins to pick up papers.

Sir.

I think it's best if you go back to your hotel and stay there.
I will notify you when we find your wife. You understand?
Please do not leave the hotel and do not leave Venice.

The POLICE CHIEF picks up his notes and leaves.

JOHN is left in the:

SMALL HOTEL ROOM

The CLERK shows JOHN the room.

CLERK: I'm afraid the room is very small, but it is quiet.

JOHN: It's fine. Thank you.

CLERK: Can I get you a drink, sir?

JOHN: Yes. A double whisky with ginger ale. No. Make that
two doubles. Thank you.

CLERK: I'll bring them up immediately.

Are you all right, sir?

JOHN: What?

CLERK: Are you all right, sir?

JOHN: No. I mean yes.

CLERK: The police will find her.

JOHN: I do hope so.

CLERK: And your son?

JOHN: I'm going to place a call now. I've hardly had time to
think about him.

CLERK: Sir. Call me if there is anything else.

JOHN: I will.

*The CLERK leaves. JOHN picks up the phone and unfolds the
paper from his pocket.*

Great Britain, please.

Hampstead 6362. It's urgent. Thank you.

JOHN replaces receiver. He takes off his shoes, gets on the bed. A radio outside is playing an English song: 'I love you, baby. I can't get you out of my mind'.

JOHN checks the phone is on the receiver properly, then closes his eyes.

A silence falls.

Phone rings and JOHN answers it quickly.

Yes. Yes.

Waits for call to go through.

Hello, Mr Hill. It's Johnnie's father, I'm just ringing to see how he is.

Listens.

Thank goodness. And no complications?

Is he sore?

Oh good. Such a relief.

What?

My wife?

I'm sorry. I don't understand. What do you mean?

Hello.

LAURA: Darling, darling, are you there?

As LAURA speaks, we see her, in England.

JOHN, shocked, says nothing. Sits up. Knocks his bag off the bed.

John? John?

JOHN: I'm here.

LAURA: It's not a very good line, but never mind. As you know, all went well. Such a nice surgeon. Luckily there wasn't much traffic and the cab got me straight there. Johnnie was just coming round when I arrived and was so pleased to see me. And you can imagine, I was even more pleased to be with him.

Such a good thing the charter ticket came up. Oh, John, it was such a funny crowd on the plane, you'd have loved them. I'll tell you all about it when you get here. Which will be tomorrow, yes? I can hardly remember what day it is today. I feel rather exhausted. All the worry and now I know he's going to be fine, I can relax.

How was your drive to Milan?

JOHN: I'm not in Milan.

LAURA: What do you mean you're not in Milan? Where are you?

JOHN: I'm in Venice.

LAURA: Venice? Wouldn't the car start? John. What happened?

JOHN: I can't explain.

LAURA: (*Suspicious.*) What's happened? You haven't crashed the car?

JOHN: (*Hesitant.*) No. No. It's nothing like that.

Pause

LAURA: You sound slurred. Did you go and get pissed?

JOHN: Laura.

(*Slow.*) I – I thought I saw you. With the sisters.

LAURA: How could you have seen me? You knew I'd gone to the airport. Really darling, you are an idiot. You seem to have got those poor old dears on the brain.

JOHN: Do I?

LAURA: You do, yes. Well what are you going to do now? You'll catch the train tomorrow, will you?

JOHN: Yes, of course.

LAURA: I still don't understand what kept you there. It all sounds very odd to me. Anyway, thank God Johnnie is all right, and I'm here with him.

JOHN: Yes. Yes.

LAURA: I'd better go. Take care of yourself and for goodness' sake, don't miss the train and drive safely.

JOHN: Yes.

Pause.

Laura. Laura.

But the line is dead.

JOHN, unable to understand, holds the receiver.

He replaces the receiver and stands up. He laughs, is slightly out of control. He picks up his bag and puts it back on the bed.

There is a knock on the door and JOHN opens it. The CLERK holds a tray and JOHN takes it.

Thank you.

JOHN takes the tray and places it down. Takes a long drink.

JOHN picks up the phone again and unfolds the paper from his pocket.

Hampstead 6362. Yes. Thank you.

He replaces the phone. Drinks whisky quickly and throws open the shutters of the window. We hear the song again: 'I love you, baby. I can't get you out of my mind'.

The phone rings and he answers it. This time we only hear JOHN's side of the conversation, which is intimate and gentle, and we only see JOHN.

Laura.

Me again, John.

No, I just needed to hear your voice again. Make sure you really are there.

I did see you.

I don't know. And I did this stupid thing, and told the police.

Well I'll have to go and see them and tell them you aren't missing.

I didn't call back to talk about that, anyway.

(*Looks round.*) I'm in a small, hot room.

I'd be able to fit you in, it'd be like the old days. Single beds and all that.

Oh, Laura. All this confusion and panic, and I keep thinking of you in the other room. It was only yesterday afternoon, but it feels an age ago.

When I get back, we'll have more nights like that.

It will all be all right, darling. Who knows what the future will bring. You are still young enough to have another, and we have Johnnie.

No. No more fights. Never.

Don't be silly. I'm fine in Venice. Forget what they said. It's you who has the old dears on the brain.

Danger? I'm not in danger. I'm not even going out. I'm staying in this small room.

I'll get the train in the morning. First thing I promise. I can't wait to see you.

Yes.

And I love you.

(*Laughs.*) No. I really love you.

JOHN holds the receiver in his hand, then replaces it. He sits on the bed.

We see the SISTERS being taken to the police station.

There is a knock on the door and the CLERK enters.

CLERK: Sir. Sir.

JOHN: Yes.

CLERK: The police are here, sir.

JOHN: Here?

CLERK: Yes, here. They ask for you and say will you go to the station.

JOHN: Oh.

CLERK: No need to worry. It is good news.

He says they have found the sisters.

JOHN: Oh no.

CLERK: But, sir. Maybe they know where your wife is.

JOHN: I see.

CLERK: So this is good, no?

JOHN: Look, I don't know how to say this.

I have just spoken to my wife.

CLERK: You've spoken to her. Where is she?

JOHN: England.

CLERK: England? I don't understand.

JOHN: No. I don't imagine you do.

CLERK: Sir, what is happening?

JOHN: Frankly, I haven't a clue. All I know is she is fine and safe and I can stop worrying.

CLERK: And what about the sisters? And the police?

JOHN: I don't know.

CLERK: You will have to go with them. They're waiting.

JOHN: Yes.

I suppose I will. Right. Come then, let's go and get it done.

JOHN leaves with the POLICEMAN.

POLICE STATION

A POLICEMAN is with the SISTERS.

The SISTERS stand and wait. Eventually,

SISTER: How long do we have to wait?

No response.

My sister has not been well.

No response.

She needs medication. She needs rest.

POLICEMAN sighs and writes.

There really can't be any reason to keep us here like this.

JOHN enters.

JOHN: There has been a terrible mistake. I don't know how to apologise to you both.

POLICEMAN: Why you apologise?

JOHN: My wife is in England after all.

POLICEMAN: Your wife in England? What you say?

JOHN: I spoke to her just now on the telephone. She isn't missing.

POLICEMAN: No missing.

JOHN: (*To SISTERS.*) It's all my fault. Mine entirely. The police are not to blame.

SISTER: But we don't understand.

The police told us she was missing.

JOHN: I thought she was.

SISTER: And they said you had filed a complaint against us.

JOHN: Oh my God. I'm so dreadfully sorry. I really thought I saw you with her.

SISTER: We said goodnight to her at dinner last night.

JOHN: I know.

SISTER: And we have not seen her since.

JOHN: No. I know that now.

SISTER: My sister is not very strong. She was considerably disturbed.

I had to plead not to be dragged off, as though we are criminals. Can you imagine? Criminals.

JOHN: A mistake. A frightful mistake. This is dreadful.

SISTER: We have been in our pensione all afternoon.

I told them this a dozen times, and they refused to listen.

JOHN: This is just too dreadful.

POLICEMAN: You finish?

POLICEMAN holds up the statement.

So you say wife in England.

JOHN: I'm afraid so. Yes.

POLICEMAN: So this document, it lies.

JOHN: Not lies exactly.

POLICEMAN: But it no speaka the truth?

JOHN: Look, I believed it to be true at the time.

POLICEMAN waits.

I would have sworn in a court of law I saw these women with my wife.

POLICEMAN: You not in court of law.

JOHN: I know.

POLICEMAN: You in police station.

JOHN: I know where I am.

POLICEMAN: You sure?

JOHN: Of course.

POLICEMAN: So who is it you see in green coat?

JOHN: I don't know.

POLICEMAN: If these signorine in pensione all afternoon, who two signorine you see? Eh? Who signorine?

JOHN: I don't know.

Look, my eyes, they deceive me. I think these signorine, with my wife, but no.

My wife, no.

My wife in England. These signorine in pensione.

POLICEMAN: *God save me from tourists.*

So all work for nothing. All men looking for wife and sisters. Men leave no stone as it sits. Men ask questions to people.

JOHN: I know. I know.

POLICEMAN: You know how many works men have to do.

Men got to catch murder. Men run after sisters instead.

JOHN: I know.

POLICEMAN: Men run round Venezia after sisters like, like cloud of ants.

JOHN: Look, I sorry for all problem. I sorry.

POLICEMAN: Know what think? Think you have too many red wine and see signora. Maybe you see a hundred signora in green coat.

A thousand signora in green coat.

[Absolutely ridiculous.]

Understand? Ridiculous.

[God give me strength.]

JOHN: Look, I feel terrible.

POLICEMAN: Good. At least that make me happy.

Pause.

This serious matter. Signorine make complaint.

Very serious matter. (*To SISTER.*) You want make complaint?

SISTER: No. No. I quite see it was all a mistake. Our only wish is to return at once to the pensione. My sister must get back.

POLICEMAN: (*To JOHN.*) Then you lucky man.

JOHN: I truly am so sorry. And please apologise to your men.

POLICEMAN gestures in despair. He leaves.

(*To SISTER.*) Please, at least allow me to see you both back to your pensione.

VENICE STREET

JOHN and the SISTERS stand outside the pensione.

SISTER: Will you come in? I am sure we can find you some coffee.

JOHN: No, thank you. I must leave you to get some peace.

I just want to make quite sure you understand what happened.

It's quite unbearable to think you could be treated like criminals.

SISTER: You have already apologised.

JOHN: But it isn't acceptable. I am afraid I have behaved very badly.

I really would like to say something now that we are here.

SISTER: Of course.

During the following, JOHN speaks with a new tone – of clarity and simplicity.

JOHN: You see, I know I saw the two of you with Laura. She looked distressed, and you were comforting her. You had your arm around her. And your sister held her other arm.

I did wonder if it had been a hallucination, but I knew it wasn't. You see the three of you were as clear to me as you are now.

SISTER: I see.

JOHN: I got into a terrible state. But I want you to understand all of this was because of my worry for Laura. She has been so fragile, and susceptible.

SISTER: We understand. We knew as soon as we saw her.

JOHN: Of course.

Since our daughter – You see I know we have a son, but this daughter –

She meant so very much to us. It is a deep wound. Very deep. We have both been greatly affected by what has happened to us.

Pause as JOHN regains control.

I'm sorry. So sorry.

SISTER: Please don't.

JOHN: I truly believed I had seen you.

SISTER: Perhaps it was an example of second sight.

JOHN: But to see Laura like that. I mean here when she was on her way to England.

Perhaps I'll never understand.

It has never happened to me before.

SISTER: Not consciously perhaps. But many things happen
of which we are not aware. My sister felt you had psychic
understanding. She did try to tell you.

Are you leaving Venice now?

JOHN: I drive to Milan in the morning to get the train.
I'm going to go straight to the hotel…

JOHN turns to the BLIND SISTER.

I hope you are not too tired.

The BLIND SISTER becomes agitated.

I'm desperate to get back to England. To my son.
And Laura, of course.

The BLIND SISTER stares at JOHN.

BLIND SISTER: You did see us. And your wife too. You saw the
three of us together.

JOHN: Yes. I did.

BLIND SISTER: But you didn't see us today. You saw us in the
future. You understand?

JOHN: No.

BLIND SISTER: It was a vision of us in the future.

The future.

JOHN turns to the SISTER.

JOHN: What does she mean?

BLIND SISTER: You must leave Venice.

JOHN: I am leaving. In the morning.

BLIND SISTER: No. Leave now. You have to leave now. Get
out of Venice.

SISTER: She's going into a trance.

Come on.

BLIND SISTER: (*Cries out.*) No. No. The child. The child. I can see the child.

JOHN: What is it?

BLIND SISTER: Her voice, I can hear her.

She is opening her mouth.

JOHN: Is it Christine?

BLIND SISTER: Her voice. The child is telling you –

The child is telling you –

The SISTER takes the BLIND SISTER's shoulders and holds her.

SISTER: That's enough. Stop.

The BLIND SISTER collapses in the SISTER's arms.

JOHN: My God. What did she mean?

SISTER: I don't know.

JOHN: What can it mean, I saw you in the future?

SISTER: I don't know.

JOHN: It is Christine she can hear. It is, isn't it?

SISTER: I have to take her in.

JOHN: But what was she saying? What was Christine saying?

The SISTER takes the BLIND SISTER away into the pensione.

JOHN is left alone.

Silence.

JOHN hears a CHILD's panicky breathing. Then her voice.

VOICE: Daddy. Daddy.

Help me.

JOHN spins round, looks. He hears the music, 'I love you, baby. I can't get you out of my mind'.

He hears the WAITER's voice:

WAITER: Don't look now.

I said don't look now, but have you seen the child?

JOHN looks round.

Don't be too obvious, darling.

JOHN sees the figure of the CHILD in her hood.

He hears the other WAITER.

WAITER: The child's body in your arms. Was it a dead weight, sir?

A dead weight.

JOHN sees the shadow of a man. He sees the CHILD. She is breathless, panicking.

What about this one?

Can you save this one?

JOHN looks around. He battles with his instinct, then makes a decision.

JOHN: Don't. Leave her alone.

For God's sake leave her alone.

JOHN chases, runs to help.

The CHILD enters the room and closes the door. She lowers her hood and we see she is the DWARF. She stops, listens. Takes out her knife.

JOHN enters the room. The DWARF puts on her hood and crouches in the water, sobs. She is the CHILD again.

JOHN slams the door, locking himself in.

It's all right. I won't let him hurt you.

It's all right.

It's all right.

JOHN approaches slowly.

JOHN holds out his hand.

Come here.

JOHN opens his arms and the DWARF runs towards him and he gathers her in his arms.

Christine.

Christine.

So, so beautiful.

JOHN pulls down the DWARF's hood and she laughs and stabs JOHN in the throat.

There is loud hammering on the bolted door and shouting.

POLICE CHIEF: [Police. Open up.]

Dogs barking.

POLICE CHIEF kicks down door.

The two other POLICEMEN arrive.

The POLICE move slowly towards JOHN who is dying.

We see the conflation of present and future:

The SISTERS appear with LAURA, exactly as before. LAURA is in her green coat and is distressed. The SISTER has an arm around her shoulder. BLIND SISTER holds her arm.

JOHN realises.

JOHN: The future. The future.

The scene continues simultaneously with the action in the present as JOHN dies, and the POLICE approach him.

The three women enter JOHN's bedroom.

LAURA picks up JOHN's jacket and looks through the pockets. She takes out his passport and looks through it, gets his wallet. She folds his jacket carefully, stroking the fabric.

LAURA sits on the bed, hugs the jacket.

They wait.

SISTER: Are you ready?

LAURA nods, but doesn't move.

Laura, dear.

LAURA: (*Very slow, very careful.*) I didn't tell you, but the other day, after the shock of finding out I was back in England, John rang me back for a second time and we talked.

Pause.

We talked about this room, this single bed he would have slept in. How we had shared a single bed once, when we first met.

And he spoke of the future. The future. Of the hope it would bring.

He meant another child. I know he meant that.

LAURA stands.

But here we are in the future, where John saw us. And look what it has brought.

Me, back here, to collect his things.

To collect his body and take it home.

Pause.

As you told him, there are things we do not know.
There are sounds we can not hear. Colours we can not see.
Vibrations. Understandings.

Pause.

We think we know everything, but there is so much more out there than the here and now.

Pause.

Thank you so much for coming with me.

I couldn't have done it without you both.

LAURA picks up the bag, very slowly looks around for the last time. Long wait, then:

All I am left with is this one thought which comes to me over and over.

All I can think is, what a bloody silly way to die.

What a bloody silly way to die.

We hear a choir: English music, young male voices.

Underneath the singing, the sound of funeral bells, and English churchyard, birds.

By the same author

Bedlam
9781849430524

Glass Eels
9781840027532

Comfort Me With Apples
9781840026337

The Farm
9781840023299

WWW.OBERONBOOKS.COM

Follow us on www.twitter.com/@oberonbooks
& www.facebook.com/OberonBooksLondon

www.ingramcontent.com/pod-product-compliance
Ingram Content Group UK Ltd.
Pitfield, Milton Keynes, MK11 3LW, UK
UKHW020737280225
455688UK00012B/709